Run, jump, skip and climb!
How do you **exercise**?

Do you play a sport?
Do you ride a bike?

sing

on

en, MD, and
Ann Nolte, PhD

ork • Minneapolis

Text copyright © 2006 by Lerner Publishing Group, Inc.

This book was first published in the United States of America in 2006.

First published in the United Kingdom in 2008 by
Lerner Books,
Dalton House,
60 Windsor Avenue,
London SW19 2RR

Website address: www.lernerbooks.co.uk

This edition was updated and edited for UK publication by Discovery Books Ltd., Unit 3, 37 Watling Street, Leintwardine, Shropshire SY7 0LW

Words in **bold** type are explained in a glossary on page 31.

British Library Cataloguing in Publication Data

Nelson, Robin, 1971-

Exercising. - (Pull ahead books. Health)
1. Exercise - Juvenile literature 2. Exercise - Physiological aspects - Juvenile literature
I. Title
613.7'1

ISBN-13: 978 1 58013 400 2

Printed in China

Do you jump a rope?
Do you walk your dog?

There are many ways to exercise.

Every time
you move
your body
you are
exercising.

Everybody needs to exercise. Exercise keeps our bodies **healthy** and strong.

When you exercise you are using your **muscles**. Your muscles make your body move. The more you exercise the stronger your muscles get.

Your muscles need **energy** to work.
Where do you get energy? You get
energy when you eat healthy food.

You get energy when you get enough sleep.

You also need **oxygen** to exercise.
Oxygen is in the air that you breathe.

That is why you start to breathe deeper and faster when you exercise. Your body is trying to get more oxygen to your muscles.

Your heart is
a muscle. It
pumps blood
around your
body. The
blood carries
energy and
oxygen.

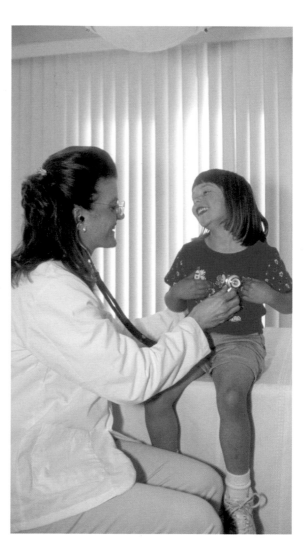

Exercise is good for your heart. It keeps your heart strong. It helps your heart pump blood.

Did you know that your body loses water when you exercise? It loses water when you sweat. Sweating helps you to cool down.

Remember to drink water before, during and after exercise. Start drinking water even before you feel thirsty!

What else should you do before you exercise? You need to stretch! Stretching loosens up your muscles so that you won't get hurt.

Stretching after exercise keeps your muscles from getting stiff. If you forget to stretch, your body might ache the next day!

To stay healthy you should exercise at least 60 minutes every day.

You can do your hour of activity throughout the day.

You could ice-skate or play tennis.

You could swim or dance. You could go hiking or play football.

You can exercise alone or with a friend.

You can exercise indoors or outdoors.

Exercise can be fun! It can make you feel good about yourself.

It also makes
you stronger.
Exercise
helps keep
you healthy!

Exercise Tips

- Drink lots of water before, during and after exercise.

- Walk or jog for a few minutes before you stretch your muscles.

- Stop exercising if you feel sick or really warm.

- Do different kinds of exercises each day.

- Get up and move around at least once an hour.

- Walk or cycle to places whenever you can.

How Do You Exercise?

How many of these things did you do today? What other kinds of exercise did you do?

athletics
badminton
biking
building a
  snowman
canoeing
climbing
cricket
cycling
dancing
flying a kite
football
Frisbee
gardening
golf

gymnastics
hockey
hopscotch
ice skating
karate
netball
playing catch
playing in the
  playground
pull-ups
push-ups
rollerblading
rounders
rugby
running

skateboarding
skiing
skipping
sledging
squash
swimming
swinging
tag
tennis
tug-of-war
volleyball
walking
yoga

More about Exercising

Books

Llewellyn, Claire. *Your Body* (Look After Yourself) Franklin Watts Ltd, 2004.

Royston, Angela. *Get Some Exercise!* (Look After Yourself) Heinemann, 2003.

Royston, Angela. *Why Do We Need To Be Active?* (Stay Healthy!) Heinemann, 2006.

Senker, Cath. *Exercise and Play* (Health Choices) Hodder Children's Books, 2007.

Spilsbury, Louise. *Why Should I Get Off the Couch?: And Other Questions About Health and Exercise* (Body Matters) Heinemann, 2003.

Waters, Fiona. *Exercise* (What About Health) Hodder Wayland, 2004.

Websites

BBC Schools
   http://www.bbc.co.uk/northernireland/schools/4_11/uptoyou/

Welltown
   http://www.welltown.gov.uk/menu.htm

Glossary

energy: power within your body that lets you move and be active

exercise: moving your body so that your muscles keep or increase their strength

healthy: being in good condition physically and mentally or something that helps you stay in good condition

muscles: parts of your body that help you move

oxygen: a gas in the air that you breathe and that is necessary for life

Index

Photo Acknowledgements

The photographs in this book appear with the permission of: © Ariel Skelly/CORBIS, cover; © Royalty-Free/CORBIS, pp 3, 4, 6, 10, 28; © age fotostock/SuperStock, pp 5, 18; Brand X Pictures, pp 7, 8, 20, 21, 23; © David Turnley/CORBIS, p 9; © SuperStock, p 11; © K. Solveig/CORBIS, p 12; © Richard Cummins, p 13; © Diane M Meyer, p 14; © Lawrence Migdale/Photo Researchers, Inc., p 15; © Gary Kufner, p 16; © Mark Clarke/Photo Researchers, Inc., p 17; © Todd Strand/Independent Picture Service, p 19; © Chris Fairclough/Discovery Picture Library, p 22; © Tom & Dee Ann McCarthy/CORBIS, p 24; © Tony Demin/CORBIS, p 25; EyeWire by Getty Images, pp 26, 27.